IMAGES of Canada
SAINT JOHN'S NORTH END
1864–1975

To Oakie the best-looking pitcher after Bobbie Shanz

Jess

Aug. 27/08

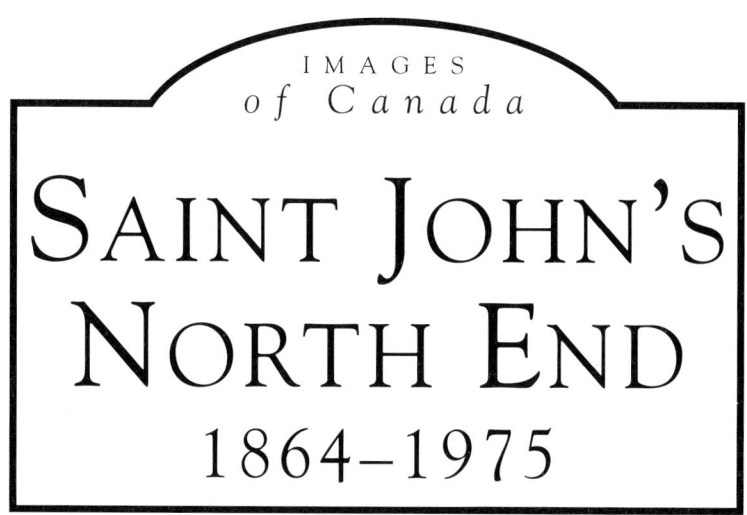

IMAGES of Canada
SAINT JOHN'S NORTH END
1864–1975

Harold E. Wright and Paul James

First published 1997
Copyright © Harold E. Wright and Paul James, 1997

ISBN 0-7524-0462-8

Published by Arcadia Publishing,
an imprint of the Chalford Publishing Corporation
One Washington Center, Dover, New Hampshire 03820
Printed in Great Britain

Library of Congress Cataloging-in-Publication Data applied for

John James (1915–1982)

Everyone called him Jack, which he didn't mind at all but there were occasions when he thought John was more appropriate. He was a child of the Great Depression, and like most men he had to hustle just to make a living. Though he very much wanted to go to college, he was obliged at age nineteen to leave his books and ship out on a freighter, and for the next two years he worked as a ship hand. Jack, as they say, was "born, bred and buttered" in the North End and upon his return he lived in the family house on Clarendon Street. It was time to look for employment once again.

In his favor he possessed three strong qualities: he could work with his hands, he could read and was well read for a common man, and he made sure any task he was given was done properly. The jobs he took read like a litany of scarce opportunities and hard times. He worked at the Comstock, Olands Brewery, and the Golden Ball. He sharpened skates, did carpentry work, and for a year or so he had his own business, "J.J. Taxi." While working for Roy Black's furniture store he studied for his mortician papers, and for the next dozen years he was an undertaker.

Then a heart attack forced him to again look for something new—a tricky business when you're forty-five with a family. For a short time he was a broadcaster on CHSJ TV and radio. But it was now that he finally got a break.

He secured the position of assistant tourism director and later, until he retired, he was the public relations officer for the city. Here was something that smacked of true work. He could now return to his books—he had always spent his extra change on books: histories, theologies, good fiction. He loved Chaucer, Dickens, Belloc, and Chesterton, and held special affection for Dr. Johnson. Johnson's society of epigrammatic friends delighted him and gave him hope. The constant habits over the years of hard work and thoroughness could now be enlisted in the pursuit of histories and their expression in words. My father wrote a clean, crisp, coherent prose.

If a cynic is an optimist gone sour he was never that. One learnt early that to whine was a mortal sin. He fought hard to maintain integrity in a world that tries to make you knuckle under. He was a hell of an example to follow and I only hope that he wouldn't mind my writing this, though brief and a bit rushed, and that he would approve.

P.J.

Contents

Dedication: John James (1915–1982)		4
Acknowledgments		6
Saint John's North End: 1864–1975		7
1.	Indiantown	9
2.	Sports	23
3.	Public Buildings	33
4.	Shipbuilding	43
5.	Domestic Architecture	47
6.	Streetscapes	53
7.	Millidgeville Airport	65
8.	Water Water Everywhere	71
9.	Rockwood Park	77
10.	North Enders	85
11.	Businesses	95
12.	Main Street	103
13.	Urban Renewal	125

Acknowledgments

This book has been a collaboration of many people. We thank the following: Dick Leonard, Don McGuire, Liz Darling, Fred Roberts, Carl White Jr., Grace Long, Charles Pratt, Lillian and Joe Logan, and the many friends and acquaintances who shared photographs with us; the staff at the Information Centre of the Public Library and the Archives of the N.B. Museum; Rick Smith, Rob Roy of Rob Roy Reproductions, and Kevin Sheehan at Appleby's Digital Imaging Centre, who digitally restored some of the photographs using their Kodak Digital Enhancement Station.

The photographs document the North End from 1864 to 1975. Sometimes a circa (c.) date is used—indicating that the precise date is unknown, but should lie within five years of the date stated. [Square] brackets indicate the date of the photograph. (Brackets) after the caption indicate the source of the photograph. The abbreviations used in the photograph credits are as follows: PANB—Provincial Archives New Brunswick; NAC—National Archives Canada; Coll.—collection; PIRP—Partridge Island Research Project. If we have inadvertently omitted somebody, our apologies. We are responsible for any errors of fact.

We dedicate this volume to Paul's father, Jack James. When Harold began his career in history, Jack provided insightful advice and guidance which remains with him today. Paul's dedication to his father appears on p. 4.

Harold E. Wright and Paul James
November 1996

Saint John's North End
1864–1975

The "North End" of Saint John is a neighbourhood—it is also a state of mind. Like all neighbourhoods everywhere the North End, like the ancient rock on which it is built, is an outcrop of its history. Those people who call it home are the expression of that history and they call themselves North Enders.

Portland, named after William Henry Cavendish Bentinck (1738–1809), the third duke of Portland, was a town quite separate from the municipality of Saint John. On its councilmen were conferred all legislative, executive, and judicial duties and conditions of an elected official. Their office included fire and police protection, the surveying of lots for business and private use, rents, the lighting of the streets, sewage, the construction of schools, the maintenance of streets and roads and their extension—in short, the multitude of common and necessary tasks that must be done to direct and service a growing and bustling community. In 1871 Portland was incorporated; by 1883 was it granted municipal status and came then to be called the City of Portland. It was in 1889 that Portland and Saint John amalgamated, thereby encircling its harbour waters with the full industry of a port city.

If the North End had a centre it was most certainly Main Street—and if ever "main" was aptly applied to name a thoroughfare it was here. It follows the simple form of a steep hill with the crest at the corner of Douglas Avenue. Running east to west it begins at the corner of Paradise Row and Mill Street and travels about a mile and a half to stop in Indiantown at Bridge Street on the Saint John River. Yet the scant distance is always hard to accept because of the thousands of people who lived and worked and played here. The grand mix of activity all crammed together along its wonderful length—the hundreds of long, narrow, clapboarded and shingled tenements with their flat tar and pebble roofs, the bakeries, restaurants, cobblers, tailors, drugstores, grocers, and fire station, the library, banks, churches, pool hall, movie theatres, back alleys, streetcars, buses, and the "Forum"—all this was the spark of liveliness that gave the North End its energy and style.

From Main Street the three lesser main streets struck out. To the south went the Straight Shore (Chesley Drive, with its shipyards and fishing huts) and Douglas Avenue (where the elegant and the ordinary house abided in unique harmony). To the north branched Adelaide Street, which hairpinned onto Millidge Avenue; here, except for the RKYC and a few homes and cottages by the rivers, there was only hinterland, the perfect spot to put an aeroport.

From the late 1920s through to the mid-1960s the North End was the centre of most of the major sporting events held in the city. There was speed skating at Lily Lake, hockey, short-track speed skating, and boxing at the Forum, senior baseball and football at St. Peters park, senior basketball and top rank bowling at St. Peters Recreational Centre, rugby and track and field at the old Shamrock Grounds, and sailboat racing on the Kennebecasis at Millidgeville. A contemporary promotion could justly call the North End at that time a sports complex. Here you had concentrated between the Forum and the Shamrocks—less than four blocks of easy walking distance—a multitude of sporting and recreational activities that you could watch or participate in. You could still swim in Marble Cove in the 1950s. St. Peters and the Shamrocks were flooded for skating and hockey in the winter and their fields and many others were occupied by kids playing games in all seasons. If you didn't have a car you took the streetcar or bus or you walked; nothing was that far away or that expensive then.

It might be considered dangerous to try to assess the distinct character of the North Ender as compared to a West Sider or South Ender or someone from the East Side. But any resident of any of the four main parts of the city knows that there is something of an alteration, a shading of the type between us, and we welcome it and are proud of the difference. Except for a few notable exceptions the North End was not the home of the "hoy poloy."

The spirit of the old North End can still be caught here and there around a kitchen table on a Saturday night perhaps, but with urban expansion and change that spirit has diminished as the old ties were broken. To not know something of your background, your heritage, your history, is to wander through life surprised at every little change that might befall you.

While these photographs concentrate on the area around Main Street, Indiantown, and the sporting activities in those areas, we have selected the original boundaries of Portland to further define the North End: beginning at the north side of City Road, north to the Kennebecasis River, west to the Reversible Falls, and east as far as the Marsh Creek bridge.

So with these photographs then let us remember for a while the old North End.

Jack worked at a variety of skilled and semi-skilled jobs over the years. In the late 1930s he was asked to ferry a truck on the back of another truck from Chicago to Saint John. This was no mean feat in those early days of poor highways. He knew after he had done that, that he had the confidence to master any job that might come his way.

One
Indiantown

Indiantown, by W.H. Bartlett, 1841. At the right is Otty & Crookshank's sawmill at Spar Cove. Indiantown received its name from the Indian trading house, built about 1779 near the corner of Bridge and Hammond Streets. Indiantown's boundaries include Bridge Street, Main Street up to the Public Stairs, Hammond Street, and Robertson's Wharf and Square. Some include Pokiok within this boundary. (Gerry Leonard family)

Another Venice? This is the Court Block, c. 1887. People are boating to their doors. Notice the wood barge between the buildings. William E. Gunter's general provision store was in the second building from the left. Gunter was a partner in the Gunter and McMulkin Mill at the foot of Kennedy Street. (Gerry Leonard family)

The Indiantown waterfront, c. 1908. The first St. John riverboat, the *General Smythe*, was outfitted at Indiantown in May 1816. The last riverboat, the MS *D.J. Purdy*, made her final trip here in September 1946. The Indiantown waterfront was home to riverboats, scows and barges, tugs, ferries, and sundry other water craft. (PIRP #2328)

The steamboat *Sincennes*. The *Sincennes* was destroyed by fire in 1911, but was rebuilt and named after D.J. Purdy, a prominent grocer, merchant, and M.L.A. The SS *D.J. Purdy* retired in 1923, being replaced by the motorship *D.J. Purdy*. The SS *D.J. Purdy* was the last side-wheel steamer to run a regular service from Saint John to Fredericton. (PIRP #4359)

The *Hampstead*. Built in Hampton in 1894, she was the first screw-propelled passenger steamer on the St. John River, and made daily round trips between Indiantown and Hampstead. She later served Wickham and Fredericton under Captain Fred S. Mabee. The *Hampstead* was destroyed by fire in 1916. (Gerry Leonard family)

The *E. Ross*. This was the ferry between Indiantown and Milford. She was built by Elijah Ross, a member of the famous Paris Crew, in Carleton in 1892, and she made several trips daily under her owner and operator, James H. Leonard. Behind the *E. Ross* is the riverboat *Aberdeen*. (Gerry Leonard family)

The area of the waterfront known as the "Bedroom." The three vessels are the *Champion*, the *Lilly Glasier*, and the tug *Admiral*. (Gerry Leonard family)

A photograph of the "Bedroom" showing P. Nase & Son's grocery and hardware store and some tugs. (Gerry Leonard family)

Indiantown Hill, located on Main at the corner of Holly Street. Charlie Pitt's barbershop was in the second building on the right. Started by his father Harry in 1879, Charlie closed the shop in 1979. George Hoben's drug store at the corner of Holly Street advertised "Hoben's Catarrh [sic] Cure always cures" and "Hoben's Tape Worm Remedy." Hoben began in 1884 in the Main Street Union Hall where Welsford's Drug store later located. (PIRP #2315)

Gault's Groceteria at 15 Main Street. Top: Louis Leonard (left) and his brother Dick stand in front of the store when it was owned by James Gault, c. 1940. Bottom: Their father Gerry (left), shown here in May 1960, bought the store from James' son Harold. Bert Long is next to Gerry. Gerry closed Gault's in September 1969. (Gerry Leonard family)

Main from Bridge Street. C.B. Pidgeon's boot and shoe store is at the left. Pidgeon is best remembered for the success of his son Walter, a Hollywood actor. The third building at the left later became Gault's Groceteria. Alexander Paterson began his business across the street in 1875. His store claimed "Everything is marked at the lowest prices consistent with a living business, and the newest styles and fashions are always to be obtained here, of the best quality." (NAC)

Gault's grocery. James Gault opened his first store in Van Wart's old shop on Bridge Street and then moved into Nase's old stand on Main Street, one building up from Pigeons. Gault (standing at center) is surrounded by Tom Hart, Margaret McElroy, and Gerry Leonard?, as well as the goods of his trade—food, hardware, and clothing. He eventually relocated further up Main (Dave Smith)

The Ferris Hotel, originally located on Bridge Street. After being destroyed in the 1899 fire, the Ferris was rebuilt at 68 Main Street, on the corner of Kennedy. It was operated by William and Theresa Ferris, and later by their son Blake and his wife Estelle. The family also had an interest in the riverboat *May Queen*. The building, which still stands, became the Ferris apartments by 1953. (Ferris Coll., #7429)

Employees of the Toronto Shipbuilding Co. at Robertson Square in 1943. During World War II several small warships were repaired at Indiantown. Marjorie Denton is the first lady on the left in the second row; her grandfather Merle is behind her in the third row with goggles on his head. (Denton Coll., PIRP #7460)

Operations at the Pokiok quarry. In 1936 Charles V. Billie got the contract to repair the Negropoint breakwater to Partridge Island. The stone was cut from the quarry, placed in a barge, and towed to the breakwater. (PIRP #7513)

The Stetson & Cutler Mill at Spar Cove. The "Big Mill" operated from 1867 until it closed in 1923. Originally built for Robert Rankin & Co., it was purchased by Hayford & Stetson (later Stetson & Cutler) in 1881. Water from the mill's boilers came from Newmans Brook. Stetson & Cutler also operated the lime kilns at Pokiok. Frederick C. Beatteay was manager of the mill. He was followed by his son, C. Allan Beatteay. (Gerry Leonard family)

McGuire's store at 1 Spar Cove Road. Top: The store c. 1904. From left to right are Mary, Harriet, Art, and John McGuire. Bottom: The store in 1965. McGuire's was first operated by Owen McGuire about 1860, and it remained in business until his great-grandson Bob closed up shop about 1970. The City later bought the building and demolished it about 1978. Behind the store was Newmans Brook, filled in to allow the expansion of Shamrock Park. (Don McGuire)

Newmans Brook. Originating at Howes Lake on Sandy Point Road, the brook empties into the river at Spar Cove. With the construction of the Rifle Range housing after World War II and the new Shamrock Park II, the waterway was filled in and the brook now runs through a pipeline. The only evidence left that it existed is the section between the Bridge Street bridge and the river, showing the pilings from the old wharves and mills. (Don McGuire)

The annual springtime ritual of flooding. This area, the Court Block, c. 1887, consisted of buildings constructed of both wood and brick. P. Nase & Son were grocers and hardware merchants. After the Court Block was destroyed in the 1899 Indiantown fire, Nase moved across the square to 1 Main Street. (Gerry Leonard family)

The spring freshet with the Eastern Canada Coastal Lines MS *D.J. Purdy* in rear, c. 1935. At the left of the photograph, partially submerged, is a gas pump. Also note that the streetcar track has been blocked off at the water's edge by a timber. (PIRP #838)

The spring freshet in Robertson Square, March 1936. The drinking fountain in the square was erected in 1883, a gift of ex-Portland Councillor & Mrs. James T. Kennedy of Marble Street, in memory of their son, A. Wilmot Kennedy, who died on October 30, 1877. (PIRP #585)

The freshet of 1923, one of the largest on record. To the left of Pidgeon's shoe store is the Riverview Hotel. The house on the hill was for many years the home of Deputy Police Chief Stephen Spinny. (Long Coll., PIRP #7260)

Two
Sports

St. Peters ballpark, c. 1923. St. Peters Church administered to both the spiritual and athletic needs of the North End from the 1920s until the 1960s. Many North End kids headed to the outfield to retrieve that elusive home run ball—for some, this was their first baseball. (Darling Coll., PIRP #7509)

The Roses ball team at Shamrock Park, 1895. From left to right are as follows: (front row) Tip O'Neill, batboy Efie Corbert, captain Frank Fanjoy, Wes Friars, Harry Black, and Ned Corey; (back row) groundskeeper Tom Hayes, ? Kelly, Billy Drummer, Walter "Shinty" Chase, H. Niles, Jack Hayes, Billy Kelly, Billy White, coach Joe Morris, Billy Curran, Jim McLeod, and manager Dr. Roberts. In September 1895 Joe Morris, "a fine all round player and always a favorite with the crowd," died after falling from a roof on Orange Street. (Don Smith Coll., PIRP #5019)

The St. Peters Junior baseball champions, 1928. From left to right are as follows: (front row) Eddie Butler, M. Gillen, and G. McCarthy; (middle row) B. Rooney, Walter Butler, E. Gibbon, J. Howard, Frank Logan, and Tommy Lifford; (back row) Joe Garey, J. Kennedy, W. Scott, Johnny Lifford, G. Burgess, and C. Rogan. (Darling Coll., PIRP #7465)

Safe! The "pick-off" play didn't quite work. The Saint John Boosters were an American import league team playing against a team from Blacks Harbour. The only Saint John Boosters player was Joe Breen. The first base ump is legendary Clem "Oakie" O'Connor. (James Coll., PIRP #7519)

Home run congratulations! Pitcher Phil Miller of the Saint John-St. Peters team has just hit one out, c. 1957. Other players from left to right are #4 Art Cunningham, #7 Billy Donovan, #5 Bob Fullton, either Fred Elliot or Sonny "Hush" Norstrom, and umpire Murray Shanks. Behind the fence near the gate are Art Scott, Vince Nowlin, Billy Fitzgerald, and Art McCarthy. (Bill Donovan)

The St. Peters senior ball team, 1961. This was the second year of renovations to the ball park. The team is standing on Nig Tracey's stands, which were built where the old clubhouse stood. The clubhouse was torn down in 1960. From left to right are as follows: (front row) Peter Murray, Sonny Norstrom, Frankie Price, Billy James, owner and manager Nig Tracey, Billy Donovan, and Berny Mackin; (centre row) Neddy Parsons, Jimmy McLaughlin, Art Cunningham, Clint Armstrong, and Bob Gallery; (back row) George James, John Hornyack, Greg Brown, trainor Pat Cunningham, Bobbie Fullerton, and Doug Foster. (James Coll., PIRP #7521)

The original Shamrock Park, c. 1956. The park was originally located where the Fairview Plaza (now Lansdowne Plaza) stood. During the summer it was used for track and field and baseball; during the winter it was used for hockey. The clubhouse was brought in from Millidgeville airport. (James Coll., PIRP# 4440, 4442)

The "fearsome threesome"—Logan speed skaters Willie, his brother Frank, and their father Fred at Lily Lake, c. 1917. Between the three they held maritime, national, and international junior and senior championships and world records. In 1932 Willie was the first New Brunswicker to win an Olympic medal, a bronze in the 5,000 meter. (Darling Coll., PIRP #5008)

Charles "The Dynamo" Gorman, the legendary international speed skater. There are stories that tell of Charles being crippled by shrapnel during World War I, and how he regained the use of his legs by skating. Military medical records do show that he was wounded in the left leg on September 10, 1918, and returned to duty on November 23, 1918. At the World Meet at Lily Lake in 1926, he was trailing the pack with two laps left to go, but began "travelling on the outside passing everyone." He won—and became the new world champion. Unfortunately, at the 1928 Olympics his medal hopes were dashed when a skater fell in front of him during the 500 meter event. The Dynamo retired soon after. (Darling Coll., PIRP #7492)

About to get sacked! Quarterback Joe Desmond of the Saint John Wanderers is shown here just before being tackled by a member of the Shearwater Flyers from PEI at St. Peters, c. 1955.

The Wanderers football team, a popular attraction at Shamrock Park in the 1950s and '60s. In 1962 they won the Burchill Cup and the N.B.-P.E.I. league championship. From left to right are #74 Carl White, #82 Bob Fawcett, #75 Bill Keleher, and #79 unidentified. White continued to play into the mid-1960s with the Saint John-Lancaster Ti-cats. (Carl White Jr.)

Provincial Champions. The King Square Credit Jewellers were softball champions in 1955–56. Shown here in front of the clubhouse at the original Shamrock Park are, from left to right, as follows: (front) bat boy John O'Toole, son of owner/coach Eddie O'Toole, and Elva (Martin) McLean, who later claimed some success as an athlete; (middle row) Donna Friars, Marlene (Mason) Vaughan, Shirley (Davis) Gallery, Betty (Davis) Martin, Patsy (Davis) Knowlen, Joanne Randel?, and Madelaine Randel; (back row) owner/manager Eddie O'Toole, Betty Richie, Alice (Haynes) Logan, Pauline Lawton, Shirley Ricketts, and co-coach Pete Friars.

The St. Peters Saints basketball team, 1948. The Saints beat out UNB and Halifax for the Maritime Junior championship at the rec. centre. From left to right are George Boyle, Al Hayden, Larry Lawlor, Bill McConn, Doug Hausen, Speed Gaines, Ray Killan, Don Sullivan, Ed Legett, Bill Dykeman, Dud Coffill, and Al Sinclair. (James Coll., PIRP #7523)

The Forum—THE place for hockey, boxing, and wrestling. Built in 1923, it was destroyed by fire in 1967. "Who could forget a cold night bus ride or walk to the Forum to watch the 'Beavers'? The crowds lining up on the ashes, breath puffing out in front of their noses, the snow banks, a soft yellow from the lights, the smell of the Forum when you entered, a strong perfume of burnt onions and hamburgers from the counters laced with a whiff of ammonia from the plant and the smell of the cold. You had to bring something to keep you warm and it wasn't always a blanket. Between periods maybe over to Kelly's for a coke or a coffee." In 1939, 5,000 fans watched the Beavers defeat the Sydney Millionaires to capture the Maritime Senior Hockey Crown. They recaptured the Maritime Crown in 1953. Over the years the appearance of the Forum changed as the metal siding rusted. (NB Pub. Coll., PIRP #3986)

The Atlantic All Stars versus Solly's at the old Forum, c. 1955. Top: Frankie Hamilton has just let loose a shot onto net. Bottom: Solly's Leon Evans is at the far right. At this point in the game Solly's was ahead 2–0. Solomon Goldberg, owner of Solly's Mens Wear on Mill Street, was a well-known sports promotor in the 1950s. (James Coll., PIRP #7524, 7525)

Three
Public Buildings

The Dominion Meteorological Observatory on Douglas Avenue, built in 1913. It provided weather information for both shipping and air traffic until 1952 when the building became home to the Saint John detachment of the RCMP. The tower and weather vane were removed in 1952. The observatory was demolished about 1975. (James Coll., PIRP #7527)

The Victoria Skating Rink on City Road. Opened in 1865, the rink was demolished in 1928. Besides ice and roller skating, it was used for concerts and exhibitions, such as the 1875 Manufacturers and Mechanics Exhibition. After the Great 1877 Saint John Fire, the rink housed hundreds of homeless people. The Colonial Inn Motel stands in its place today. (Hall Coll., PIRP #2403; James Coll., PIRP #7526)

The Vocational School. Designed by Saint John architect F. Neil Brodie, the building was built in 1925–26, and classes began in September 1926. The school's motto is "Train Mind and Hand, Learn to Live." In May 1942, Shakespeare's *A Midsummers Night Dream* was staged with Kay Smith as director. (James Coll., PIRP #7528; Fred Roberts)

The fifth grade of Alexandra School, 1946. Located opposite Victoria Square, the school opened in 1899 and closed in 1976. It reopened as Senior Citizens Housing in 1980. In the photograph are Rosemary Day, Neil Banks, Richard Colwell, Evelyn White, Ruth MacPherson, Donnie Gilson, Billy Chisholm, Kathleen Williams, Marilyn O'Neill, Louis Stillwell, Paul Legette, Donnie McRitchie, Donald Harvey, Lorne Ferris, Donald Laurie, and Fred Roberts (second row, third from left). (Fred Roberts)

The King George School on Bentley Street. Built in 1911 by John Mooney & Sons, this school, like many older inner-city schools, eventually closed, and was demolished in 1988. (Thomas Coll., PIRP #2327)

Holy Trinity School. John Flood & Sons built the school in 1922–23. The excavation for the foundation is shown here, in a photograph that is testament to the term "manual labour." The home in the background was built in 1864 for Isaac Burpee, who "spared no pains in making this house all that can be desired as a first-class, comfortable and cosy residence." It is now the Mount Carmel Convent. (PIRP #4444)

The current St. Peters Church. The first mass was celebrated here in December 1884. This church replaced the old church on Magazine Street and was the centre of Roman Catholic life in the North End. St. Peters was also the centre of sports life for the community in the 1950s and '60s. (PIRP #2801)

The Zion Church. This house of worship was constructed in 1858 by John Owens, a prominent Portland shipbuilder. After the church closed, the building was reopened in 1885 as the Owens Art Institution, the first public art gallery in Canada. It became the parish hall for the Holy Trinity Church until the 1950s, when it was demolished for the expansion of Holy Trinity School. (PIRP #6768)

The Zion Church (left) and rectory on Burpee Avenue and St. Paul's Church on Wall Street. St. Paul's Chapel opened in 1842 as the Chapel of Ease for St. Luke's Church on Main Street. It became a parish church in 1856 and was torn down for a new church in 1869. (Dr. George Bate)

St. Paul's (Valley) Church, designed by architect Matthew Stead. The cornerstone was laid in September 2, 1869. By 1912 the upper portion of the spire had been rebuilt and the tower restored. In 1933 the spire was covered with fireproof shingles. In July 1981 workers began removing paint from the old wooden building using blow torches. The subsequent spectacular fire destroyed a most historic and impressive church. (Dr. George Bate; St. Paul's Church)

Portland Church. After being destroyed in the North End fire of October 1877, the church was rebuilt. Slightly less than one hundred years later, on July 3, 1970, demolition of Portland began again, this time as part of the Urban Renewal program. As before, the church was rebuilt, this time on Millidge Avenue. It reopened for service on September 27, 1970. (Kilcup Coll., PIRP #6924)

No. 3 Hook & Ladder company, 23 Portland Street, 1907. The station was across the street from Portland Church. Suspended from the bar are helmets and lanterns. The fire hall also doubled for a time as the North End lockup. (Ferris Coll., PIRP 8048)

No. 5 station at 302 Main Street. This station opened in 1898: "The front will be quite imposing. It will rest upon five granite piers, joined by arches. The facing will be of pressed brick, while the front window on the upper story will be coped with red freestone. A neat copper cornice will give an effective finish to the whole." [1897] This station provided the primary fire protection for most of the North End until No. 8 station opened in Millidgeville in 1964. No. 5 was recently replaced with a new station a short distance from this site. (Ferris Coll., PIRP #8013)

No. 4 station, City Road, c. 1940. From left to right are as follows: Lieutenant Dow, John Porter, Joe Little, Gordon Campbell, Bill Galley, and Captain Hoyt. In their 1937 report, the N.B. Board of Underwriters wrote that the condition of No. 4 hall "is poor" and that it should be replaced by a central station on Carmarthen Street (this finally happened about forty years later). The equipment here included a La France hose and chemical truck, and an Amoskeag steamer, put in service in 1877. (Ferris Coll., PIRP #8077).

Four
Shipbuilding

The *Rock Terrace*. David Lynch launched this ship from his yard at the Mill Pond (now the Tim Hortons location on Main Street) in June 1875. The *Rock Terrace* was the first vessel owned by Troop & Sons, one of the largest shipping fleets in Saint John history. In January 1888 she hit a coral reef outside Guam. Unable to reach harbour, the crew abandoned ship. The abandoned vessel sailed on for another five months before she went aground off Tarawa. (Lynch Coll., PIRP #6814)

The 1894 launching of the pilot schooner *David Lynch* at the Hilyard shipyard (the foot of Harrison Street where the new HMCS Brunswicker building stands). The shipbuilder was David Lynch. In the background is Douglas Avenue. (Lynch Coll., PIRP #6807)

The steamship *Senlac* in the Hilyard shipyard. David Lynch built this vessel for William Thomson & Co. The carpenters were supplied by George V. Beatteay. The *Senlac*, launched in January 1904, served the coastal route along the south shore of Nova Scotia, PEI, and Newfoundland. She was destroyed by fire in 1915. To the right of the yard was McCready's Vinegar Pickle Works. (PIRP #3160)

The four-masted schooner *Dornfontain*, launched on June 11, 1918, from the Straight Shore (where Ocean Steel is today). Enroute to South Africa she was captured by a German U-boat in the Bay of Fundy and set afire. (Fowler Coll., PIRP #6530)

The *Ada A. McIntyre*. After being launched at Moss Glen on the Kingston Peninsula on September 25, 1918, the *Ada A. McIntyre* was brought to Indiantown for outfitting. She was lost off the coast of Maine in 1923. (McIntyre Coll., PIRP #3978)

David Lynch's home at 141 Paradise Row, *c.* 1900. Prominent shipbuilders such as David Lynch lived in houses which were testament to their successes. Originally built for shipbuilder John Owen, Lynch had this house "thoroughly remodelled, the ceilings made higher, rooms enlarged, staircases improved . . . another story, or Mansard roof . . . added, with projecting tower and lookout." [1881] Lynch, from Londonderry, was probably the best of all the New Brunswick shipbuilders. His grandson, Charles Lynch, the well-known *Southam News* columnist, was born here. The building was demolished in 1975 for the Garden Street overpass expansion. (Lynch Coll., PIRP #6742)

Five
Domestic Architecture

Belvidere Hall, popularly known as Reeds Castle. Located on Mount Pleasant Avenue, this home was built between 1854–56 for Robert Reed, a prominent shipbuilder: "The grounds of Mr. Robert Reed . . . are fast assuming shape and comeliness. The garden in front, is at the moment in full bloom. Flowers of every fragrance pervade the atmosphere far and wide. We never saw a piece of ground made so much of, converted into so many beautiful shapes as this parterre in front of the Gardner's Lodge." [1856] Reed converted his home into the Mount Pleasant Hotel, and it was later used as the Sacred Heart Convent. It was demolished in 1913. (New Brunswick Museum)

Count Robert Visart deBury's home, 354 Main Street, *c.* 1946. Count deBury, vice-consul for Belgium, built this Second Empire house in 1875. The ceilings in the double parlors "were dominated by the great roses of plasterwork from which the chandeliers were suspended, and by the heavy, ornate cornices . . . the cove of the cornice was shaded in pink and rose . . . The open areas were festooned with garlands of roses painted in delicate greens and pinks, with a light, free brush-stroke." (Armstrong Coll., PIRP #6834)

Samuel Taylor's home, 266 Rockland Road, *c.* 1899. This Carpenter Gothic home was built between 1847 and 1861. Taylor came to Saint John in 1846 from Donegal, Ireland. Samuel's great-grandson, Shirley Kitchener Taylor, born January 21, 1899, is shown here being held by his mother, Elizabeth Hamm. The other lady is Annie Saunders Taylor, Shirley's grandmother. In 1980 the house was demolished for the Garden Street overpass extension despite efforts from the Taylor family to have the house moved. (Taylor Coll., PIRP #7462)

Clifden Terrace, a Gothic Revival stone house on Parks Street. This home was built in 1856 for William Parks of Buckley, Ireland, a prominent ship owner and businessman. He was president of the Commercial Bank of New Brunswick and the Western Extension Railway, and founded the New Brunswick [Cornwall] Cotton Mill, the first cotton mill in British North America. He died with the sinking of the SS *City of Boston* in 1870. (New Brunswick Museum).

Ringwood (left). Built in 1856 for James Reed, brother of Robert, it was later owned by Howard P. Robinson and then K.C. Irving. To the right is the home of Franklin Stetson, owner of the Stetson & Cutler Mill. Stetson bought this house about 1890 and in 1959 sold it to Irving. It was demolished to make the public garden across from Ringwood. Lily Lake is in the background. (PIRP #7464)

The Second Empire house at 233 Douglas Avenue. Druggist Samuel Hawker had this home built in 1920. The cast-iron fence in front of the house and the grill on the porch roof no longer exist. It is now home to plumber Brian Hickman and his family. (Hickman Coll., PIRP #2333)

The Second Empire home at 247 Douglas Avenue. This building was constructed between 1872 and 1875 for blacksmith David McIntyre. During the 1959 visit of Queen Elizabeth, most of the houses on the avenue were decorated with bunting and flags. The Thomas family lived here at the time. (Thomas Coll., PIRP #2346)

The Queen Anne home at 212 Douglas Avenue. Fred Tapley, the chief clerk of the Inter-Colonial Railway, had this house built in 1880. The Tapley family were prominent Portland businessmen and civic officials. (New Brunswick Museum)

Henry Miller's home at 158 Douglas Avenue. Miller, owner of the Miller & Woodman lumber mill in Indiantown, had this house built between 1872 and 1875, and Millers owned the house until the 1940s. The decorative iron grill, the porch, window brackets, and decorative wood siding have all been removed. The adjoining property at #170 was an identical structure. (Miller Coll., PIRP #2341)

Fraser Gregory's home at 297 Douglas Avenue. Gregory was president of the Murray & Gregory lumber mill. His house was built in 1901: "It is of wood, two storeys high, with steel shingling. The cellar contains furnace and laundry. There are five bedrooms and a bathroom; also drawing, sitting, sewing rooms, kitchen and sculleries. The front stairway and windows display excellent workmanship." [1901] The current owners, Harold and Bev Grew, have done a wonderful job of preserving the house. (New Brunswick Museum)

Six

Streetscapes

Long Wharf, Main Street, and Paradise Row, including Fort Howe, Mount Pleasant Avenue, Rockland Road, and Lily Lake, all the way to the Kennebecasis River, 1930. Note the Cold Storage building at the foot of Main Street. The site of the RP & WF Starr coal terminal is at bottom right. Today this area is but a shadow of its former self. Some might argue that it is no longer a neighbourhood. (PIRP #4127)

Wright Street and Mount Pleasant Avenue from Jeffrey's Hill (Garden Street), c. 1870. "The view presented . . . is one of busy industry—Residences advancing rapidly to completion . . . and altogether the scene recalls to the mind the operations of the Tyrian multitudes in the building of an ancient city." [1864] The Garden Street carwash would be at the bottom right of Jeffrey's Hill. (James Coll., PIRP #6146)

The Mount Pleasant Hotel, formerly Belvidere Hall (Reeds Castle), and the observatory on Mount Pleasant Avenue, with Winter and Wright Streets in the foreground. The rooftop of the Victoria Rink is in the foreground. Many of these buildings in the "Valley" still exist. (PIRP #1874)

The driveway of American Consul General D.B. Warner's home on Mount Pleasant Avenue, 1890. On the box seat is Peter Clinch and Kit Warner. The others, from left to right, are as follows: (first seat) Miss Gertrude Drury, Mrs. W.L. Busby, and Mrs. Ella Gooch; (at top) Charles E. McPherson (with feet hanging over), V.G.R. Vickers, Arthur R. Adams, and Nan Burpee; (third seat) Edith Burpee (with back toward horses) and Florence Adams; (back seat) Sheriff R.R. Ritchie, Miss Bessie Adams, and Florence McMillan; (standing rear with horn) Charles Harrison; (inside coach) Dr. Frank Esson; (standing front) Lieutenant Colonel George W. Jones and W.L. Busby. (James Coll., PIRP #586)

Skeet shooting at the old golf links, c. 1913. Princess Elizabeth School is now in this area. In the background is the old Sacred Heart Convent, formerly the Mount Pleasant Hotel. (Hughes Coll., PIRP #5020)

Sandy Point, or as it was formerly known, the Howes Road. The two children on the sled are probably in the area of the Aquatic Driving Range. They may be members of the Peacock family, who have lived in the area for over one hundred years. (PIRP #4357)

Cobbetts Well, Fort Howe, April 12, 1930, facing toward Mount Pleasant Avenue. William Cobbett was stationed at Fort Howe from 1785 until about 1788. He later became a popular English author and member of Parliament. (James Coll., PIRP #7529)

The Millidgeville ferry omnibus on Adelaide Street, c. 1920. This service may have been run by the Fundy Motor Line Ltd., managed by Clarence V. Emerson. Although the streets may be mud, the gutters are lined with granite paving blocks. (James Coll., PIRP #7530)

The Straight Shore. This area was home to many fishing families such as the Lords and Logans. It was also the site of shipyards and mills during the nineteenth century. During Urban Renewal it was realigned, rebuilt, and renamed Chesley Drive. (PIRP #2731)

An aerial view of Douglas Avenue, the Straight Shore, and the harbour, c. 1930. At the bottom left is the Thomas Hilyard home, later demolished for the construction of the New Brunswick Museum. On Bentley Street is the King George School and Dwyers bakery. The former Hilyard shipyard is in the centre left of the photograph. (James Coll., PIRP #6148)

The Battle of Paardburg memorial service, Riverview Memorial Park, February 24, 1957. The twenty-man Honour Guard from the First Battalion, Royal New Brunswick Regiment (Carleton & York) was commanded by Second Lieutenant Gerry Merrithew, later a minister of Veterans Affairs. The CSM was WO2 T.S. Fairweather. Reverend H.H. Hoyt is at the cenotaph. (James Coll., PIRP #4451)

A postcard view of Douglas Avenue, c. 1920, showing the homes across from Riverview Memorial Park. The extension of the streetcar service down the avenue in 1902 led to a building boom in this area of the avenue. (PIRP #2802)

Patchell's store at the corner of Celebration and Stanley Streets, 1902. The delivery wagon in the rear is carrying Butter-Nut bread. The store window has advertisements for Red Rose Tea and Jello. Note the gas light fixture on the pole at the right. (James Coll., PIRP #7531)

A Saint John Fire Department funeral, City Road, c. 1940. Deputy Chief Furlong is leading the firemen. At the right is the Swift Canadian Company at 89 City Road, and the City Road Bottle Exchange. Note the paving block-covered street and the streetcar tracks. (Ferris Coll., PIRP #8082)

Boyd Street, Rockwood Court, c. 1950. The cornerstone for this wartime housing project was laid by Mayor C.R. Wasson in December 1942. (PIRP #833)

Paradise Row, facing Wall Street, c. 1970. At the far end of the street was McCullums grocery, next to the Texaco station. Today this street is anything but "paradise." (Kilcup Coll., 6929)

Paradise Row and Rockland Road, c. 1973. Construction is underway on the throughway. Brenan's Funeral Home is at the left, the David Lynch house (with a white roof) is to its right, and St. Paul's Church is at the extreme right. (Lynch Coll., PIRP #6739)

A Christie Woodworking Ltd. truck moving down Second Street in front of the Lutheran church onto Cedar Grove Crescent, *c.* 1950. (PIRP #670)

The intersection at Lansdowne Avenue and Elm Street, 1967. Ed's taxi stand at 39 Lansdowne is next to the Irving station at the left, and the Fairview Plaza can be seen at the rear. The Esso station is advertising "Put A Tiger In Your Tank." (James Coll., PIRP #7532)

Portland Place, *c*. 1950. Before the war this was the site of the old Saint John Golf Links. Constructed as housing for returning World War II veterans, Portland Place has remained relatively unchanged. (Condon Coll., PIRP #5969)

Wellsley Avenue on August 27, 1952. Of the five children on the sidewalk, four are on tricycles. Behind the second girl, there is an empty tricycle with a wagon behind it. A General Bakeries Bonny Bread truck is at the right. (James Coll., PIRP #7533)

Seven
Millidgeville Airport

Millidgeville airport, operated by Atlantic Airways Ltd. The airport, opened in 1929, acquired an international reputation in the early 1930s when its facilities were used by aviators attempting to fly the Atlantic. Millidgeville closed in 1951 when the new airport at Clover Valley, Loch Lomond, opened. At the bottom of the photograph is the RKYC and the ferry landing for the *Maggie Miller*. (Boyer Coll., PIRP #310).

Otto Hillig and "Liberty." In June 1931, Otto Hillig, the "Flying Photographer," landed his grey and orange Bellanca monoplane "Liberty" here enroute to Copenhagen. The man in the centre is City Chamberlain Foster Thurston. On that same day Ruth Nichols, hoping to become the first women to fly solo across the Atlantic, crashed her Lockheed Vega at the airport. (Parfitt Coll., PIRP #5195).

Amelia Earhart with her crimson Lockheed Vega in May 1932. The day after Bernt Balchen flew the plane in, Amelia took it to Harbour Grace, Newfoundland, enroute to Londonderry. She was the first woman to fly across the Atlantic as a passenger and as a solo pilot. (Peacock Coll., PIRP #144).

The Millidgeville flying boat station. In 1920 Navy Island was selected as the site for one of Canada's permanent flying boat stations because "St. John harbour offers special advantages . . . protection from winds, facility of refuelling and proximity of proper accommodation for the visiting aviators." They obviously forgot to mention the fog, tides, and currents. The seaplane base was later established at Millidgeville in 1929. The aircraft is believed to have been owned by Bluewater Fisheries Ltd. (Ellison Coll., PIRP #433).

The oft-used Millidgeville airport. The Saint John Flying Club, local and visiting aviators, as well as airlines such as Maritime Central Airways, used Millidgeville from 1929 until its license was cancelled in 1951. In 1932 Tom McHugh and Wilfred Comeau constructed a Pietenpaul Air Camper, the first homemade plane at Millidgeville. Other well-known local aviators were Jimmy Wade, Fred Hartwick, Bill Arrowsmith, Scotty Stirley, and Rudyard Brayley (the latter two were killed in a crash in 1931). Note the aircraft model on top of the Imperial Oil wind sock. (Ellis Coll., PIRP #4874).

A Ford Tri-Motor and a Fairey seaplane from HMS *Norfolk*, part of the 1933 Maritime Goodwill Air Tour. Within two months of the airport's opening, the first air pageant was held under the auspices of the Saint John Flying Club. The second was held in 1931 with displays of parachute jumping, RCAF Sisken bombers, and an Autogiro. (Ellison Coll., PIRP #447).

The RCAF Station St. John in May 1941. On September 1, 1939, the Royal Canadian Air Force established this station at Millidgeville. The No. 2 Army Co-Operation Squadron, and No. 117 and 118 Squadrons were stationed here at various times during the war. LAC Cal Calahan is shown here refuelling a Lysander. (Calahan Coll., PIRP #2420).

Two Lysanders on patrol over Courtenay Bay. At the left is the drydock and below the aircraft is McAvity's foundry on Rothesay Avenue, both potential targets. (PIRP #312)

An overview of the RCAF Station St. John with Millidge Avenue at the top and Boers Head Road at the right. The runways are shown at the bottom and left of the photograph. The aircraft hanger still stands today on Woodward Avenue. It is home to Waypak Inc., formerly Wayside Industries. (Peacock Coll., PIRP #162)

Irving Oil's Grummand Mallard before the crash. In December 1951 this plane crashed shortly after take-off. Pilot Jimmy Wade and the plane's lone passenger, K.C. Irving, clambered out of the aircraft moments before it burst into flames. Wade, a pilot for Irving for many years, was the best known of the pilots who flew from Millidgeville. (Cail Coll., PIRP #4984).

Eight
Water Water Everywhere

The original City of Portland, surrounded by water on all sides. The Kennebecasis River is in the foreground, with the St. John River and Marble Cove at right. The harbour is at the top. Millidgeville airport is at the centre. (Spinny Coll., PIRP #5930)

The MS *D.J. Purdy* at Indiantown, *c.* 1944. The YMCA organized river cruises for soldiers and their families during the war. (Graham Coll., PIRP #4940)

A warship passing under the Reversible Falls bridge enroute to Indiantown for repair, *c.* 1944. (McPherson Coll., PIRP #6023)

The Millidgeville ferry *Maggie Miller* outside the RKYC, c. 1910. (O'Neill Coll., PIRP #2416)

Captain H.F.C. Currie (left) and deckhand A.N. Worden, of the Millidgeville ferry *Maggie Miller II*, April 27, 1954. (PIRP #7377)

Fred Robert's first boat, the *Queen*, at the foot of Kennedy Street, 1959. At the bow is Ira Marr; at left is Bobby Roberts. (Fred Roberts)

The Robert Roberts & Sons piledriver at Marble Cove. Robert Roberts & Sons operated a wharf pile-driving business for over fifty years. To hear the thumping of the piledriver was for the people around Marble Cove the first sign of spring. The old Forum is in the background. (Fred Roberts)

Marble Cove, home of the Saint John Power Boat Club for over seventy-five years. The SJPBC held annual cruises upriver to Belyea's Point (their first cruise was in August 1918). Native Americans used the cove for centuries, and had a portage trail behind the museum to the harbour. (PIRP #2799; James Coll., PIRP #4458)

The Royal Kennebecasis Yacht Club (RKYC). The RKYC was formed in 1894 and received its Royal charter in 1898. The flag officers during this 1973 spring freshet were Honourary Commodores George B. Oland and William H. Holder, former Commodore Robert L. Logan, Commodore Ralph H. London, Vice-Commodore Graeme F. Somerville, and Rear-Commodore Andre Oulton. (Charles H. Pratt)

The *Arcal* at the yacht club during the 1973 spring freshet. Charles H. Pratt tied his vessel, the *Arcal*, to the railing of the yacht club, where he and his wife Donna prepared for the upcoming boating season. (Charles H. Pratt)

Nine
Rockwood Park

"The grand formal opening of Rockwood Park takes place this afternoon at 2:30 o'clock when Mayor Sears in an address from the big pavilion will declare the various features complete and ready for enjoyment . . . [an] excellent programme of aquatic sports provided by the Neptune Rowing Club . . . with music from one of the city's best bands. A display of fireworks will be provided for the evening and those desiring to avoid a walk home and back again can procure meals or lunches at the pavilion." [1907] The pavilion was destroyed by fire in 1912. (James Coll., PIRP #7534)

Lily Lake, the jewel of Rockwood Park. In 1865 there was a proposal to create a park around the lake. Before 1877 Melbourne Goggins operated the Lily Lake House for tourists: "no city in America has within a mile and half of its business centre, so beautiful a sheet of water as Lily Lake and perhaps no people could be found anywhere who have done so little through their public authorities to make this lake available." [1894] In 1895 Lily Lake became the jewel of the new Rockwood Park, owned by the Saint John Horticultural Society. (PIRP #2752)

One of Rockwood Park's many trails, c. 1900. Trails like this led from Lily Lake to the Zoological Gardens, the Animal Zoo, the Arboretum, and to the many other lakes within the park such as Harrigan Lake and Drury's Long Lake. (PIRP #4355)

No. 1 Hook and Ladder's float of Frank White's Ferris wheel and "shoot the chutes" in the 1907 Fireman's Tournament parade. Also offered by White at his amusement grounds at the lake were "Egg Drinks and Temperance Bottled Drinks," "Ice Cream and Ice Cream Soda, College Ices, Fruit, Confectionary, Cigars and Rockwood Postal Cards." (Ferris Coll., PIRP #8031)

The zoo at Rockwood Park, 1924. "There was another younger bear in the Park that had a cage of its own near the residence of the American eagles. He walked in the straight and narrow path that little bears should tread and when he saw the winter snows approaching and his toes began to be nipped with cold, he snuggled into a corner of his cage, turned a deaf ear to the sounds of the city in the distance and passed into sweet slumber. He is wide awake now and will be promoted to occupy the premises vacated unwillingly by the big bears that would not go to sleep when they should have." There has been a zoo at Rockwood Park since it first opened. (Seeds Coll., PIRP 3541)

The Zoological Garden near the bear cage, c. 1910. "It is to spots like Rockwood Gardens that they direct their footsteps in the cool of the evening, where they can find some of the peace of the country amongst the beautiful flowers and shrubs in the sweet smelling gardens." [1908] (Doig Coll., PIRP #4633)

One of the park's riding trails, 1932. There have been miles of trails within the park since its early development. At the Rockwood Riding Academy, Alex Long (third from right), a well-known harness racer, taught many people the joys of trail riding. His daughter Muriel stands to his left, and her future husband, Johnny Watts, stands third from the left. (Long Coll., PIRP #7257)

"In 1906 . . . the Saint John Ice Company was granted the right to build an ice block conveyer, and . . . a huge structure which stretched out over the surface of the lake, and was designed to remove the cut slabs of ice from the open water . . . to the ice houses perched on the high hills overlooking the lake." In 1907 two children nearly drowned when they fell into the open water by the conveyor. (PIRP #3697).

"Shoot the chutes," an early version of today's water slide. "Several persons enjoyed a trip down the incline and all pronounced it a most thrilling feature." A motor at the top of the chute pulled the boat back up the incline. (PIRP # 3922)

Swimming at Lily Lake. In 1899 Downing Vaux, the landscape architect who designed New York's Central Park, did a development scheme for Rockwood Park. Included were plans for riding and walking trails, an arboretum, a zoo, fishing, boating, and skating, but none for swimming. Residents and visitors have been swimming at Lily Lake since before the 1830s. Top: The gents changing room and the artificial beach, c. 1930. Bottom: The diving board, c. 1920, still at the lake in the 1960s. (James Coll., PIRP #7535; Richards Coll., PIRP #5679)

Lily Lake in the 1960s. From the 1920s to the 1960s the lake changed very little. There was still playground equipment on the beach, and the old wooden boats, with their big black ID number on the bow, were still available for rent. (PIRP #599)

The new pavilion. In 1956 the Horticultural and the Fish & Game Associations financed the construction of the new pavilion. The lake was still a popular swimming spot in 1971 when the City received the Vincent Massey award for excellence in an urban environment for the redevelopment of the park, c. 1970. (Kilcup Coll., PIRP #6919)

The first artificial lake, completed in 1904 using both park staff and "hard labor jail prisoners." The purpose of this lake was to provide a steady supply of water for Lily Lake during a summer drought. The artificial lakes (there are now five), commonly referred to as the "Arches," are now called the Fisher Lakes after John Fisher, an early member of the Horticultural Association. (James Coll., PIRP #7536)

Ten
North Enders

Christmas 1903. William A. Chesley, co-owner of the Chesley Brother's iron knee manufacturer on the Straight Shore, lived on the first floor at 226 Douglas Avenue. His sister Edith and her husband Donald lived on the second floor. Donald was half-brother to Hollywood actor Walter Pidgeon. From left to right are Jack A. Chesley (later a superintendent at the drydock), Arthur S. Chesley, and Nettie A. Pidgeon (the latter two both became doctors). Nettie is holding a stuffed parrot. (Chesley Coll., PIRP #3896)

The Pokiok ice-boat, 1916. Charlie Smith built this unusual river ice-boat at his home on Pokiok Road. Shown here are John Smith (left) and Wallace Kelly. The ice-boat still exists. (Cail Coll., PIRP #4987)

The Street Railway tug-of-war team. In 1913 most of them lived in the North End. From left to right are as follows: (seated) Thomas Mitchell, motorman, Fairville; Percy Moore, motorman, 125 Victoria Street; Fred Campbell, motorman, Saint James Street; Ira Ferris, motorman, 96 Wall Street; and Leonard Armstrong, conductor, 99 Moore Street; (standing) Captain Charles B. McLean, motorman, 155 Bridge Street; coach Albert Pearson, conductor, 97 Main Street; and Lobrieski Hanselpacker, motorman, 160 Adelaide Street. (PIRP #7252)

Joe Logan on Main Street with his new tricycle, 1932. Joe does not appear very happy! If you look closely at the handlebar on his bike, you will see that it is held together with rope. A next-door neighbour broke the handlebar. (Joe Logan)

Fred Roberts, dressed as a Mountie for a play at Alexandra School, behind his home at 36 Cedar Street, c. 1946. Fred's family operated a wharf pile-driving business. (Fred Roberts)

Louis and Dick Leonard ready for a ride outside their home at 155 Bridge Street. It seemed as if every kid in the 1940s to 1960s had a wagon, tricycle, or scooter. (Gerry Leonard family)

Alex Long with his daughter Grace outside their home at 23 Lombard Street, *c.* 1940. Alex drove a delivery truck for MRA's. (Long Coll., PIRP #7259)

The James family and friends on Harvey Street. Top: Mary Ellen James holding her son, c. 1946. In the backgrounds are the flats of Harvey Street which no longer exist. Right: Jack James, owner of J.J. Taxi, with his helper on Harvey Street, c. 1948. In the background the old Forum and Kellys Restaurant can be seen. (Paul James)

Left: Janet Bate outside the rectory of St. Paul's (Valley) Church, May 1947. In the background is the corner of Paradise Row and Wall Street. Bottom: Reverend W. John Bate (Janet's grandfather), John (her brother), and Reverend Alban F. Bate (her father). Reverend W. John Bate was a pastor in Newcastle, N.B., for many years; Reverend Alban F. Bate was the pastor of St. Paul's (Valley) Church from 1936 to 1963. (Dr. George F. Bate)

Right: Druggist Benjamin P. Toal outside Wassons at the corner of Paradise Row, 1948. Toal had previously worked for Welsfords. Bottom: A few years later Wasson opened the Viaduct Brunch Bar where Marie Stirling worked. Note the Mission Church on Paradise Row at the right, c. 1952. (PIRP #4680, #4679)

Don McGuire wearing his new jersey at Newmans Brook. On every street corner, during every season, groups of kids got together for pick-up games of hockey, baseball, or football. In the 1950s Don McGuire and a few of his friends got together and formed the "Bed Ticks 6" hockey team. One of their opponents were the "Exterminators" from the drydock. Some of the other team members were his brothers and cousins Bob, Jack, Art, and Lou McGuire, John and Dave Ferris, Gino Williams, and Harold Holland. (Don McGuire)

Ralph Howlett, 1964. Howlett, an inspector for the Department of Agriculture, lived at 49 Main Street. He was the major commercial duck decoy carver in southern New Brunswick between 1920 and 1960, and carved over 2,000 ducks. Today his decoys are collectors items across North America. (Chris Howlett)

The Kashetsky family at 185 Rockland Road, 1951. From left to right are grandmother Rachel Nagelberg, Ancil, Esther, Herzl, and mother Blanche. They lived here from 1940 until the building was demolished in 1981. Herzl is a well-known painter. Not shown are his brother Joe, also a well-known artist, and their father Max, a prominent antique dealer. (Kashetsky family)

Brownies Lana and Cheryl Logan, with their sister Krista and brother Kevin, on the front step of their home at 35 Wigmore Court, c. 1969. This little group was on their way to St. Peters ball park for a parade. The scout and guide organizations were extremely popular in the 1950s–60s in the North End. The St. Pius X Church on Somerset Street sponsored brownies, guides, cubs, and scouts. (Lillian Logan)

The playground behind St. Peters ball park where children from all over the North End came to play. Top: The ball field fence, with numerous advertisements for local businesses such as Jack Calps Mens Wear, Hopper Electrical, Dowd Roofing, Baxter Dairy, and Bonds Restaurant. Behind the fence is the old Forum. Bottom: Miss Lundy, mother, nurse, craftwoman, and slide polisher for the children. (James Coll., PIRP #7537, 7538)

Eleven
Businesses

The Irving gas station at the corner of Douglas Avenue and Main Street. Originally built as Phillips grocery and bakery in 1898, it was converted to a gas station by Charles Gorman in 1930. It was later managed by Ray Conway. The building was demolished about 1988. (James Coll., PIRP #7544)

The corner of Metcalfe Street and Lansdowne Avenue. To the left of the Irving station is the Dominion store, c. 1960. (James Coll., PIRP #7539)

The corner of Metcalfe Street and Lansdowne Avenue, facing Main Street, 1967. The Cash & Carry Cleaners is now a parking lot; across the street there is now a McDonalds restaurant. (James Coll., PIRP #7540)

Ring's boat repair, c. 1953. Many North Enders operated their own small businesses. Grenville Ring followed his father Wellington in operating his own boat repair yard. Born on Portland Street, Ring specialized in the repair and restoration of old wood boats. He died in 1978. His son Bob and grandson Geodie followed in his footsteps. (Bob Ring)

Samuel H. Hawker's drug store, the corner of Mill Street at Paradise Row. The store was destroyed by fire on December 18, 1919. The second building on the left was a branch of the Bank of Nova Scotia. (PIRP #674)

Grace Long (right) in front of Hazel's store at 41 Lombard Street, *c.* 1950. (Long Coll., PIRP #7258)

The Miller & Woodman lumber mill at Robertsons Point as seen from Pleasant Point in Milford, 1874. (PIRP #2750)

Stetson & Cutler's Snowflake Lime Limited. The company operated burners at Pokiok and a quarry on Somerset Street. It is rare to see early workplace signs that state "Accidents Can Be Prevented—We Want Safe Workmen!", c. 1935. (James Coll., PIRP #7542; 4449)

Bill Leonard (left) and Perley Coleman breaking in Dwyers Bakery's new western horse, c. 1940. Dwyers was on Bentley Street. It later became General Bakery. (Gerry Leonard family)

A Butter-Nut "is good bread" delivery truck, 1940. The bakery was on Douglas Avenue from 1929 until 1975. (Byers Coll., PIRP #7447)

The Murray & Gregory Ltd. sawmill, sash & door factory, and art glass works on Falls View Avenue. Many businesses and home owners prided themselves in having products made by this company. (Priddle Coll., PIRP #6138, 6139)

The new Simpsons-Sears store under construction in the winter of 1954–55. Sobeys started shortly after. (James Coll., PIRP #7543)

Twelve
Main Street

One of the best known corners on Main. Ray Conway's gas station was across from Dr. Roberts' home, where there is a police car parked in front. Across the street was Welsford's Drug Store in the old Women's Christian Temperance Union Hall. Also located here was the Portland Public Library and the Knights of Pythias Hall. Next is the original Bank of Nova Scotia, followed by St. Lukes manse (hidden from view) and St. Lukes Church. (James Coll., PIRP #7545)

The Regent Theatre, c. 1955. The kids are lined up waiting to see "Blazing Arrows Flaming From the Screen"—the *Conquest of Cochise*. The police constable is believed to be Clifford Boyd, a west-sider, who is wisely wandering away from the howling mob behind him. (James Coll., PIRP #7546)

Main at the corner of Harrison Street. The Maritime Rug Works is at right. Joe Logan, seen earlier on his tricycle, worked here for many years. Across the street was the Lansdowne Super Market. (PIRP #4519)

Looking toward St. Lukes Church, c. 1967. The Baxter Dairy truck at left is just about where the stairs went down to Murray Street (next to the phone booth). (James Coll., PIRP #7547)

Driscoll's at Lansdowne Avenue, c. 1955. Like Welsfords and Wassons, this was a North End fixture well known for its soda fountain "floats." (James Coll., PIRP #4479)

Fred J. Watts hardware. Fred opened his store in 1925 in the block between Portland and Simonds Streets. Top: In 1928 he moved to this location and remained here until he sold the business in 1975. He sold tea cups for 5¢, Yale locks for 40–50¢, and Gillette blue blades, five for 25¢. Bottom: Fred is at the cash with one of his brothers behind him. Upstairs was one of the best toy departments in the city, with Tonka trucks and dinky toys. (James Coll., PIRP #7548; 7549)

The rotary, c. 1970. Few motorists will fondly remember rotary traffic on Main at Lansdowne. Was the main purpose of the rotary to swing vehicles and customers to the plaza? Behind the signs are Conway's Irving gas station at Douglas Avenue, O'Reilly's Meats, Rays Fish Market, and Fred J. Watts. (James Coll., PIRP #7550; 7551)

Leo Cormier's Community Market on Lansdowne Avenue, c. 1955. Although known for his meats, his window sign reads "Finnanhaddie, Smoke Mackeral, Shad, Salt Herring, Fillets,

Kippers, Boneless Cod." The store later became the Lansdowne Super Meat Market. (James Coll., PIRP #7553; 7554)

A delivery truck for the Lansdowne Super Meat Market outside the store at the corner of Lansdowne Avenue, c. 1960. This is probably the early stages of rotary traffic. There is a police officer standing next to the temporary traffic sign. (James Coll., PIRP #7555)

A Butter-Nut truck turning left onto Douglas Avenue enroute to the bakery, c. 1962. Dr. Matthew H. Cavanaugh's dental office is in the Roberts building at the right. The large number of vehicles on the street testify to the importance of Main as a major city street. (PIRP #2976)

Main at the beginning of Urban Renewal, c. 1970. Driscolls still stands at the corner of Lansdowne, but the buildings on Harrison Street had already been demolished for the Chesley Place Mall by the time this photograph was taken. (Kilcup Coll., PIRP #6908)

The Price & Shaw fire at 222 Main. Price & Shaw were carriage and sleigh makers across from the Main Street Baptist Church. They made pungs, slovens, sleighs, railway luggage trucks, and even Saint John's first ambulance. This could be their fire of May 22, 1877. The firm closed about the time of World War I. (Ferris Coll., PIRP #8122)

Shave or a haircut? Joe McIntyre's first haircut in 1973 made him the fifth generation of the family to be cut by Charlie Pitt. Charlie's father, Harry Pitt, started cutting hair in his Main Street shop in 1879. "Mr. Pitt's customers are not generally in a hurry . . . They come not just to get a haircut but to pass the time, to see their friends, to trade a few jokes, and to talk about everything under the sun." Charlie kept the shop open until shortly before his death in 1980. (Jack McIntyre)

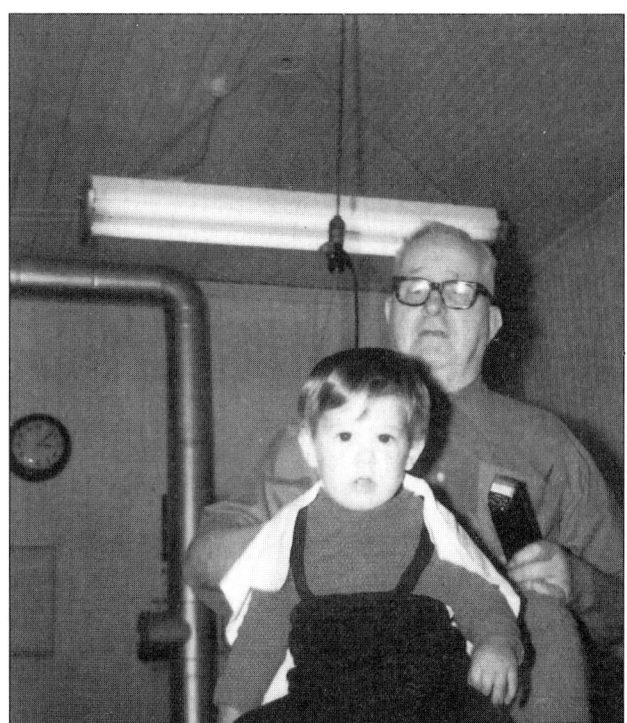

Gorman's station, Main at Douglas. In 1930 speed skater Charlie Gorman opened his second service station, the first being on Portland Street. "The new station is most attractive, with its glazed brick walls and elaborate lighting scheme. To make the station the lower floor of the building was removed, and the top story is now carried on steel beams . . . It is fitted up with all the latest machinery for speedy and accurate service. Four pumps of the newest type . . . ensure short waits for gasoline. Grease pits are provided for the greasing of cars." Primrose gasoline promised "more miles and more smiles." (PIRP #7698)

The Polymorphian's float on Main Street at the foot of Fort Howe Hill during the 1897 Diamond Jubilee of Queen Victoria's coronation. On the float are five gunners from the Portland Battery, Third N.B. Regiment of Artillery. In the background is the Boston Dental Parlor. (James Coll., PIRP #7556)

The Corkery building, c. 1925. Located at 653 Main, it included Weizel's Shoe store. "No matter how poor a store was, it boasted a canvas awning. In whatever stage of decline, it blossomed its plain or multicoloured protection in the morning, lowered by ropes and a crank, and it was folded back every night." (PIRP #4417)

The Great 1877 Fire Parade of 1932 coming down Main. On the Sunday nearest June 20, the fire and police departments held their annual Great 1877 Fire parade. The City Cornet Band is just to the right, followed by Deputy Fire Chief Bob Carson. At the foot of Elm Street was the Boston Dental Parlor. (Ferris Coll., PIRP #8123)

The block between Portland and Simonds Streets, decorated for the 1939 Royal Visit of the King and Queen. The businesses are, from left to right, as follows: Barker's Grocery, #538 Main; Lee Sing's Chinese laundry, #532; Travis Drugs, #526; Herbert G. Harrison, feed & produce, #522; and J.W. Davidson's grocery, #518. (Thomas Coll., PIRP #4247)

Gearing up for the holidays, c. 1970. Christmas decorations strung across the streets were always a welcome sight for North End kids as they knew Santa would soon follow. The businesses shown are the Liquor Store, Daves Restaurant, Grahams Restaurant and Banquet Rooms, Nickerson's Restaurant, Joyce's Food Market, Titus Bakery, and the Portland Hardware. (PIRP #4119)

Main at Portland Street from Rockland Road, c. 1970. The second building at the left is McArthur's Wallpaper, followed by North End Auto Repair, Portland Street, and O'Keefe's Food Market. (Kilcup Coll., PIRP #6905)

Main at the foot of Elm Street, 1967. The block between Portland and Simonds Streets was one of the last to be demolished. Jock Bowen kept Splanes on Main to the very end, then relocated to Kanes Corner. On Simonds Street there was Atlantic Home Improvement (new & used goods) at #18, Cash & Carry Cleaners at #36, Albert Pierce's harness and leather repair at #28, and the Kosy Corner grocer at #38. (James Coll., PIRP #7557)

Splanes, c. 1970. Located at the corner of Simonds Street, Splanes was to sporting goods what Watts was to hardware. Many a North End child got his first Mitchell fishing reel from Splanes. (Kilcup Coll., PIRP #6906)

The Bell, Book & Candle at 537 Main across from Portland Street, c. 1960. Previous to this store Morrisey Drugs and Thomas' furs were located here. After Urban Renewal the Bell, Book & Candle moved to Charlotte Street. Berny Bloom's clothing store was at the right. (James Coll., PIRP #7558)

Main and Rockland Road from Joseph A. Likely's Timber Pond. James V. Russell's boot and shoe store is visible just above the Likely building in the centre of the photograph. (Titus Coll., PIRP #6840)

Main at the corner of Mill and Paradise Row, 1918. Wasson's Drug store is at the right. The building sign at the left advertises Brandham-Henderson white lead paint and varnishes. Streetcars, sleighs, and slovens were among the modes of transportation of the day. (Lynch Coll., PIRP #6823)

Main shortly before the arrival of King George VI and Queen Elizabeth in 1939. The businesses at the right included Wasson's Drugs, Bev Appleby's National Packing, James B. Watts Public Benefit Hardware, and the Dominion Food Shops. (Thomas Coll., PIRP 4246)

The lower end of Main near the Viaduct, c. 1950. At left is Arnoff Brothers new and used goods, Stirling Electric, and further down the hill, O'Neill's funeral home. (PIRP #629)

Philip Grannan's plumbing store, across from Morrisey's Drugs. When this building was erected the words "Stoves" and "Ranges" were made part of the roofline cornice. (PIRP #4114)

Top: Ed's taxi is parked outside Morrisey's Drug store just below Rockland Road, c. 1950. Bottom: Archibald Green's tobacco store at the corner of Acadia Street, c. 1955. Within two decades everything disappeared for the construction of Hilyard Place. Gone was the Bell, Book & Candle, Grannan's plumbing, O'Neill's funeral home, Wassons, and behind the buildings, Acadia, Camden, and Chapel Streets. (PIRP #3887; James Coll., PIRP #7559)

The Viaduct, built in the early 1950s to ease traffic congestion along Mill Street to Main. On the left is the old Cold Storage. Charlie Currie worked here from the 1940s to the 1980s. Whenever there was a power outage he would take the chicks from the hatchery to his home at 17 Camden Street. At Easter the chicks would be coloured and given to kids as pets. (Kilcup Coll., PIRP #6902)

The K Grounds on August 4, 1942. During World War II the grounds were used by the army. In the foreground is the rifle range (now Churchill Boulevard), the gas training area, Newmans Brook, the Kiwanis (K) Grounds (later Fairview Plaza), and then Lansdowne Avenue and Main Street. To the left of the K Grounds is the Saint John Golf Links. (Col. J.G. Hart Coll., PIRP #1611)

Thirteen
Urban Renewal

The North End, c. 1950, prior to Urban Renewal. We can still see Shamrock Park behind St. Lukes Church, and home construction on Churchill Boulevard had not yet started. Basically everything in the bottom half of the photograph was demolished in the 1960s and '70s "all in the name of progress." Gone were Camden, Acadia, Chapel, Murray, Harrison, and Sheriff Streets, McCreadys Pickles, McCormick & Zatzman, Gars Army & Navy Surplus, the Cold Storage, the bingo parlor on Simonds Street, and Cosman's store on Chesley Street—all gone. As far as the eye can see—this was all the North End, before Urban Renewal. (PIRP #5015)

Stirling Electric being demolished, c. 1970. The 1946 Saint John Master Plan identified the worst of the slum areas to be south of Main Street from Harrison Street east to Long Wharf, plus the triangle between Main, Rockland Road, and Millidge Street. The "dwellings present a frightful fire hazard as well as abysmal living conditions." (Kilcup Coll., PIRP #6915)

The only two buildings left on Murray Street, c. 1970. At the upper left is the deBury house at the corner of Douglas Avenue. The LBR is at the left. (PIRP #4104)

Harrison Street demolition, c. 1970. (Kilcup Coll., PIRP #6912)

Main Street demolition below Rockland Road, c. 1970. (Kilcup Coll., PIRP #6914)

Right Electrical, Barny's Clothing, O'Reilly's, and Wilsons fish market, c. 1970. As properties were being purchased for demolition, fire fighters were kept busy answering arson calls. (Kilcup Coll., PIRP #6910)